For Georgia, most of this song was created
with you in my arms. —J.K.

To Angel, for always being there. —C.S.

The art was created by combining watercolor, pencil, and collage with digital painting and texturing.

Internal images on pages 36-45 credit to: Page 36, NASA/STScI; Page 37, A. Fujii; Page 38, top left: K. Rhode, M. Young and WIYN/NOAO/AURA/NSF, top right: NASA, ESA, S. Beckwith (STScI), and The Hubble Heritage Team (STScI/AURA), bottom: NASA, ESA, and the Hubble Heritage Team (STScI/AURA) - ESA/Hubble Collaboration; Page 39, left: ESA/Hubble and NASA, right: NASA/JPL-Caltech; Page 40, NASA/JPL-Caltech; Page 41, X-ray: NASA/CXC/UNAM/Ioffe/D.Page, P.Shternin et al; Optical: NASA/STScI; Illustration: NASA/CXC/M.Weiss; Page 42, NASA/STEREO science team; Page 43, left: NASA/JPL-Caltech, right: NASA/JPL-Caltech; page 44-45, from left to right: NASA, ESA, the Hubble Heritage Team (STScI/AURA), J. Bell (ASU), and M. Wolff (Space Science Institute), NASA/JPL/University of Arizona, NASA/JPL/Space Science Institute, NASA, ESA, and L. Lamy (Observatory of Paris, CNRS, CNES), NASA/JPL.

Published by Sourcebooks Jabberwocky, an imprint of Sourcebooks, Inc.
P.O. Box 4410, Naperville, Illinois 60567-4410
(630) 961-3900
Fax: (630) 961-2168
sourcebooks.com

Library of Congress Cataloging-in-Publication Data is on file with the publisher.

Source of Production: Worzalla, Stevens Point, WI, USA
Date of Production: June 2018
Run Number: 5012603

Printed and bound in United States of America.
WOZ 10 9 8 7 6 5 4 3 2 1

Twinkle Twinkle Little Star

I Know Exactly What You Are

words by Julia Kregenow, PhD

pictures by Carmen Saldaña

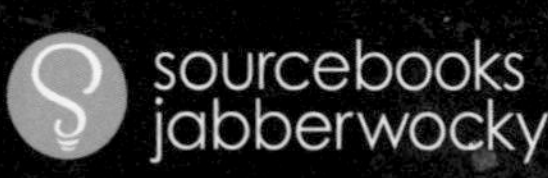

Twinkle, twinkle, little star,

I know exactly what you are.

Opaque ball of hot dense gas,
million times our planet's mass,
looking small because you're far,
I know exactly what you are.

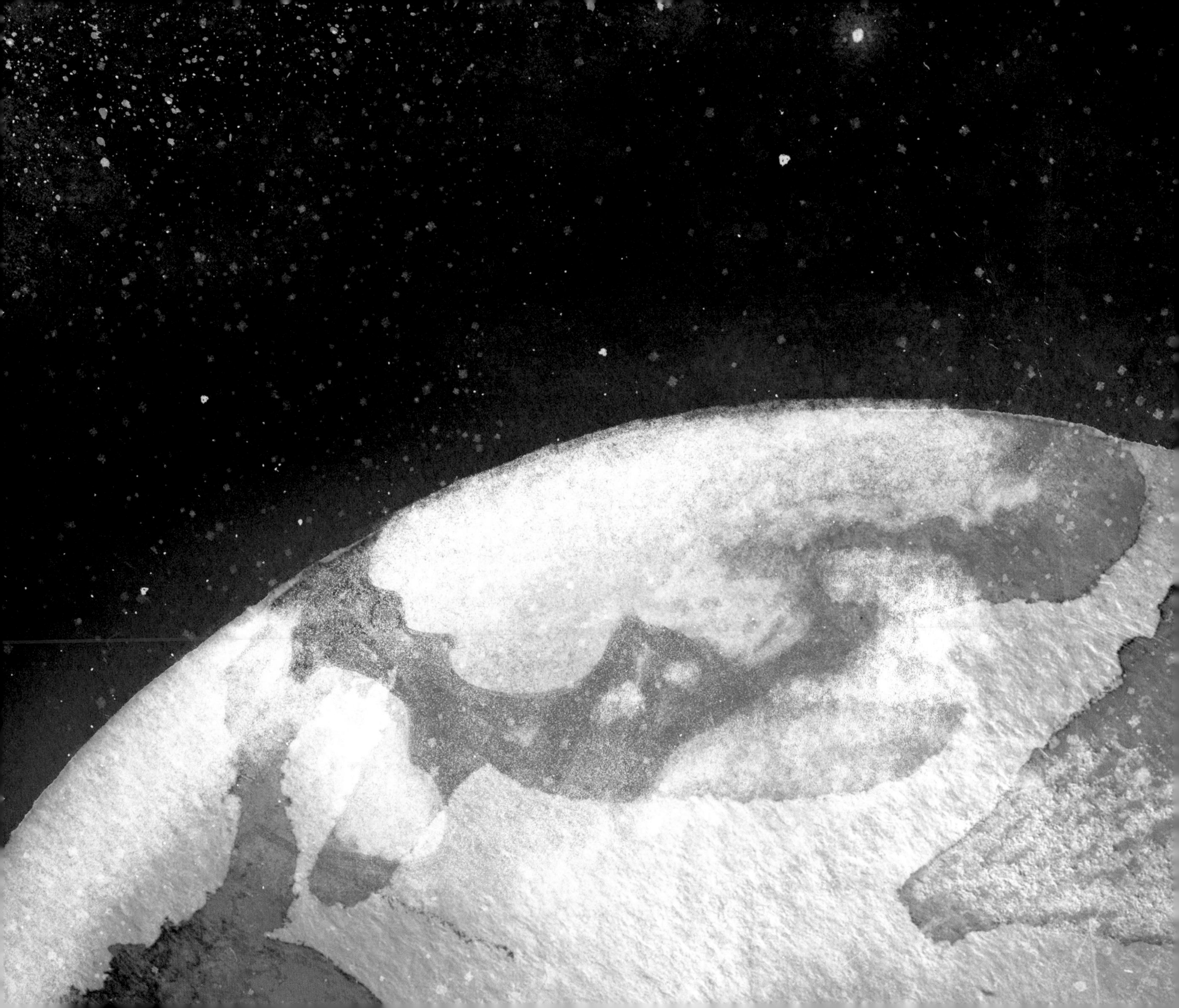

Constellations are at best just a cosmic Rorschach test. Random patterns spread 3-D, viewpoint dictates what we see.

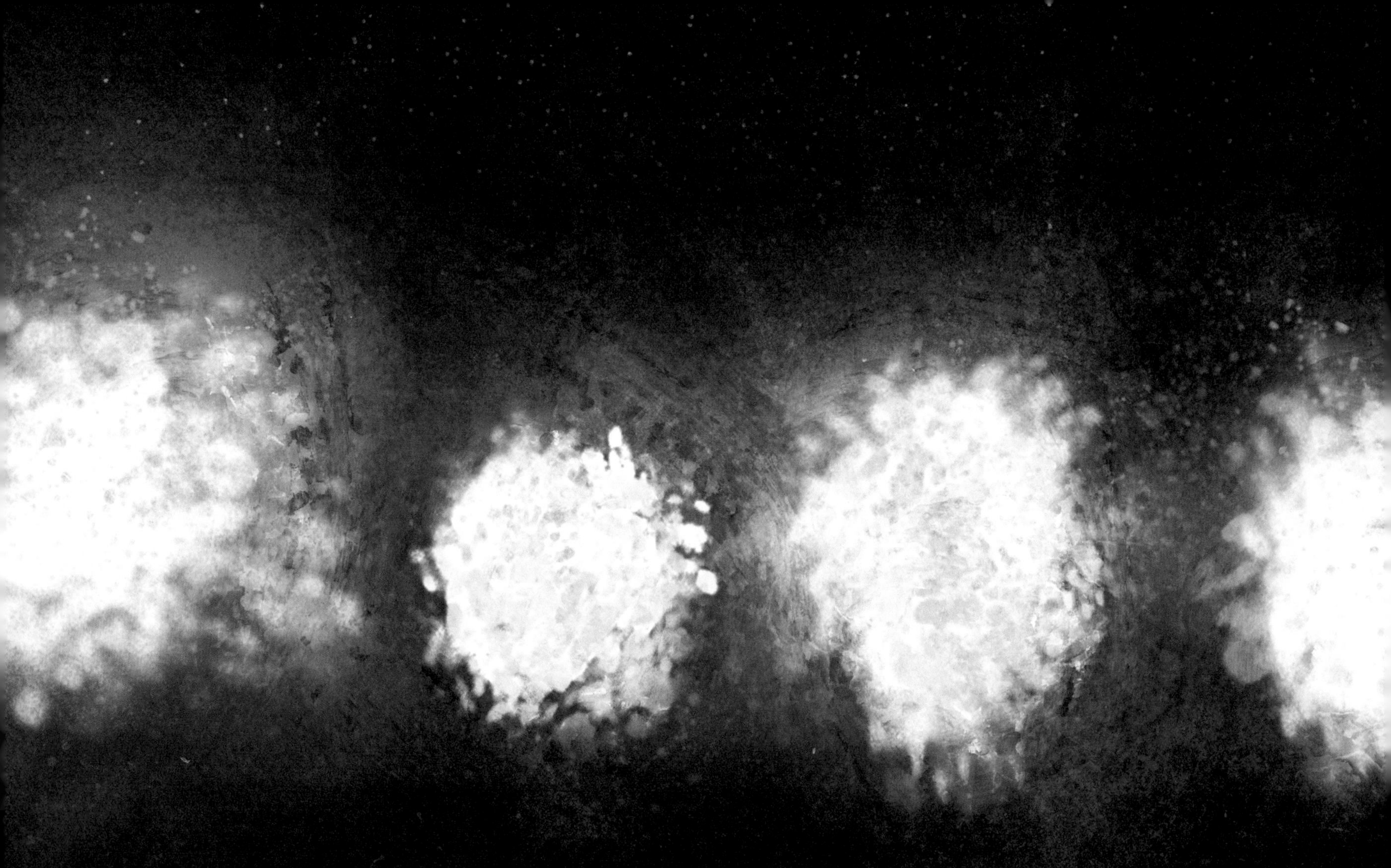

Atmospheric turbulence
causes rays of light to bend.

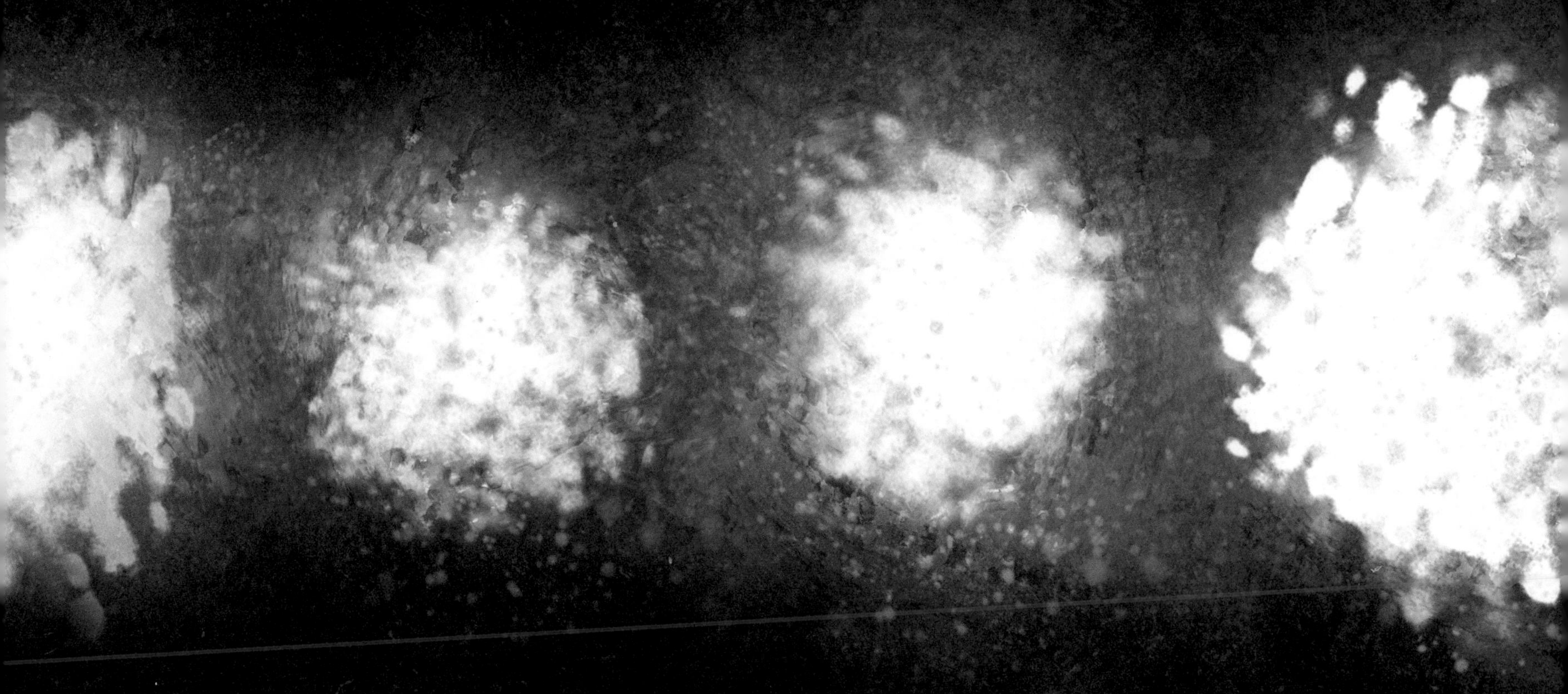

Blurry light gives views subpar
causing twinkling little star.

Fusing atoms in your core:
hydrogen, helium, carbon, and more.
With such power you shine far,
twinkle, twinkle, little star.

Smallest ones burn cool and slow,
still too hot to visit, though.
Red stars dominate by far,
twinkle, twinkle, little star.

Largest ones are hot and blue,
supernova when they're through,
then black hole or neutron star.
I know exactly what you are.

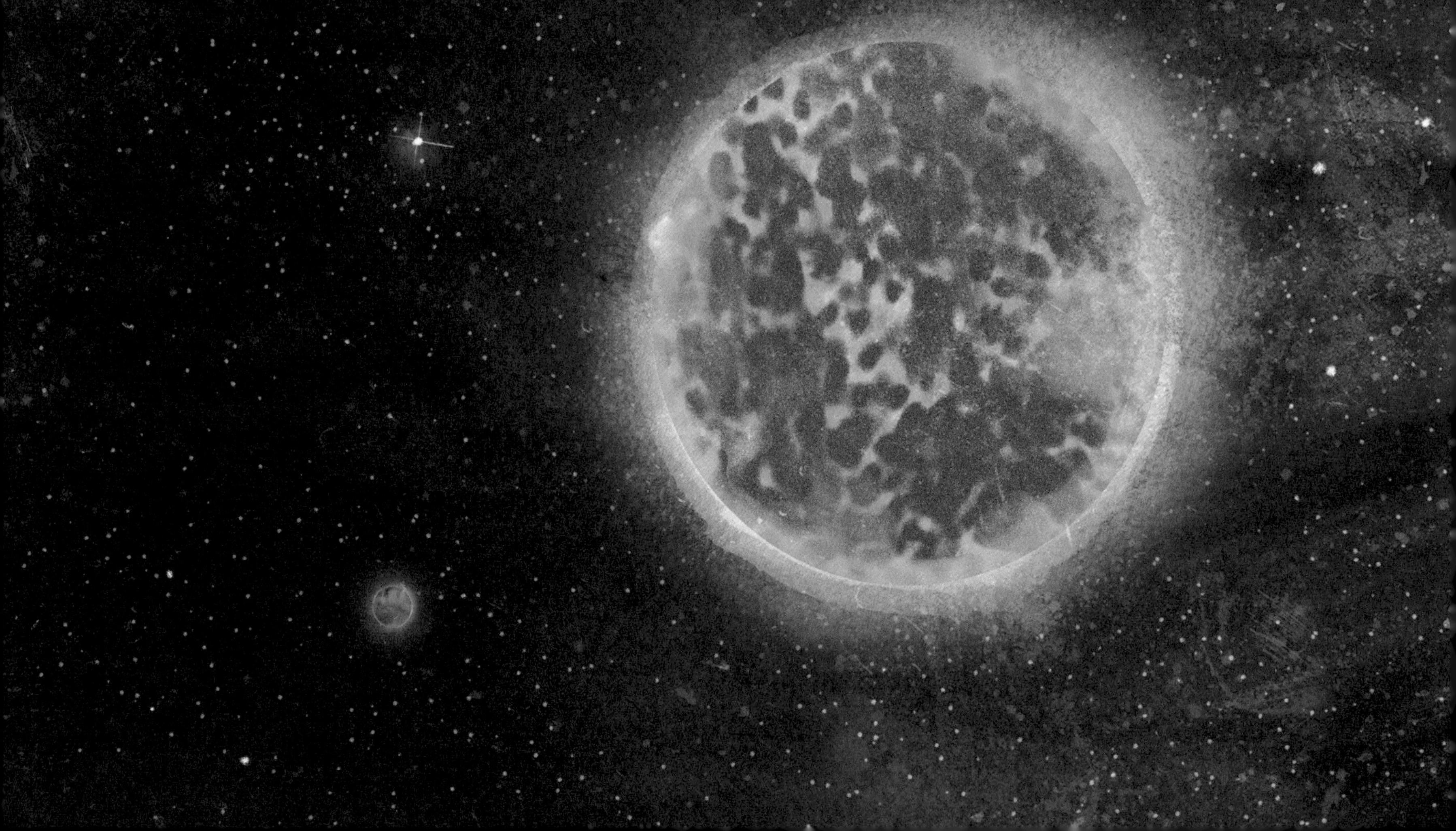

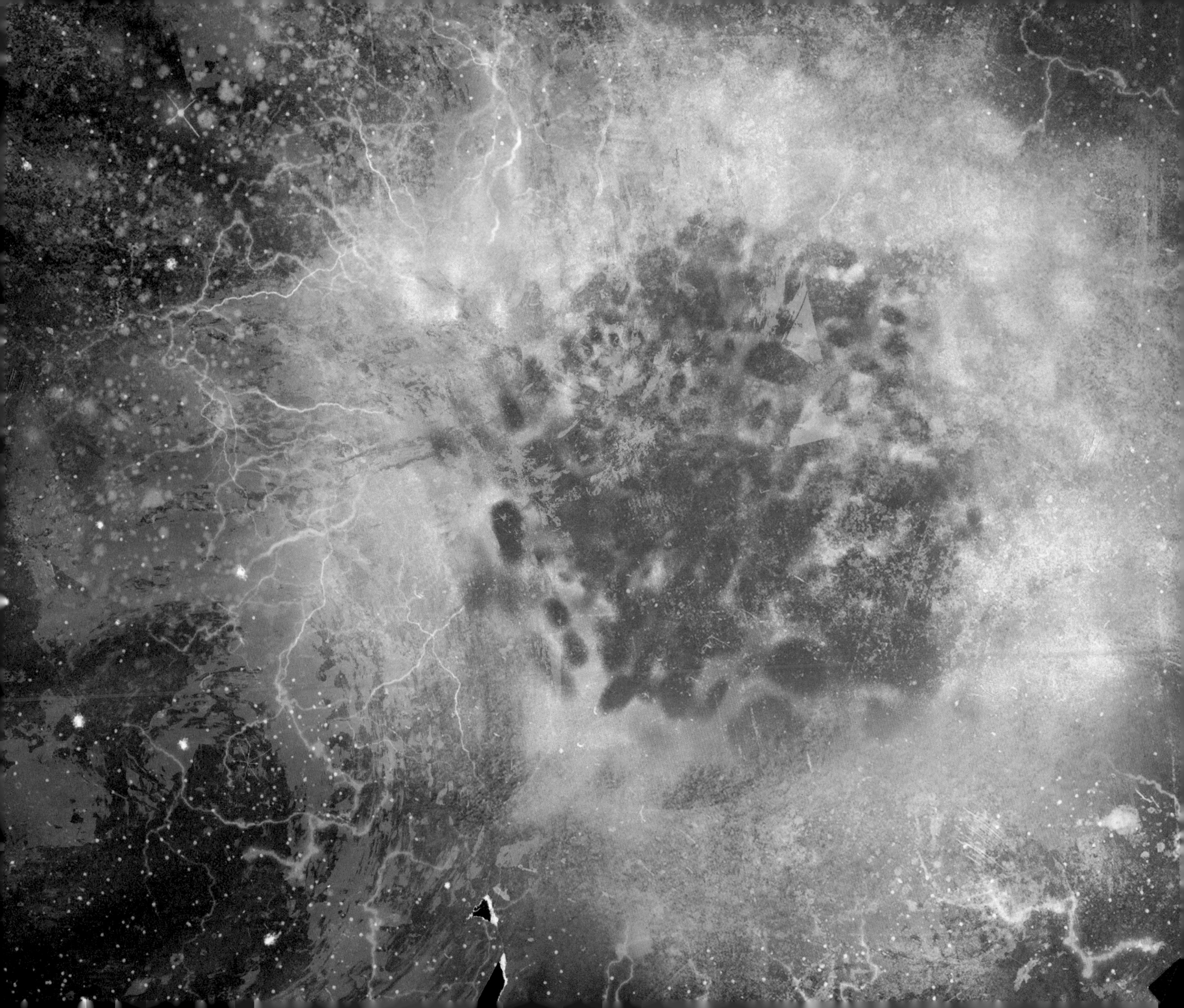

Gravity holds on too tight,
nothing gets out, mass or light.
Black holes are the most bizarre
remnants of a twinkling star.

Neutron stars spin really fast
when your beams of light sweep past,
then we call you a pulsar.
I know exactly what you are.

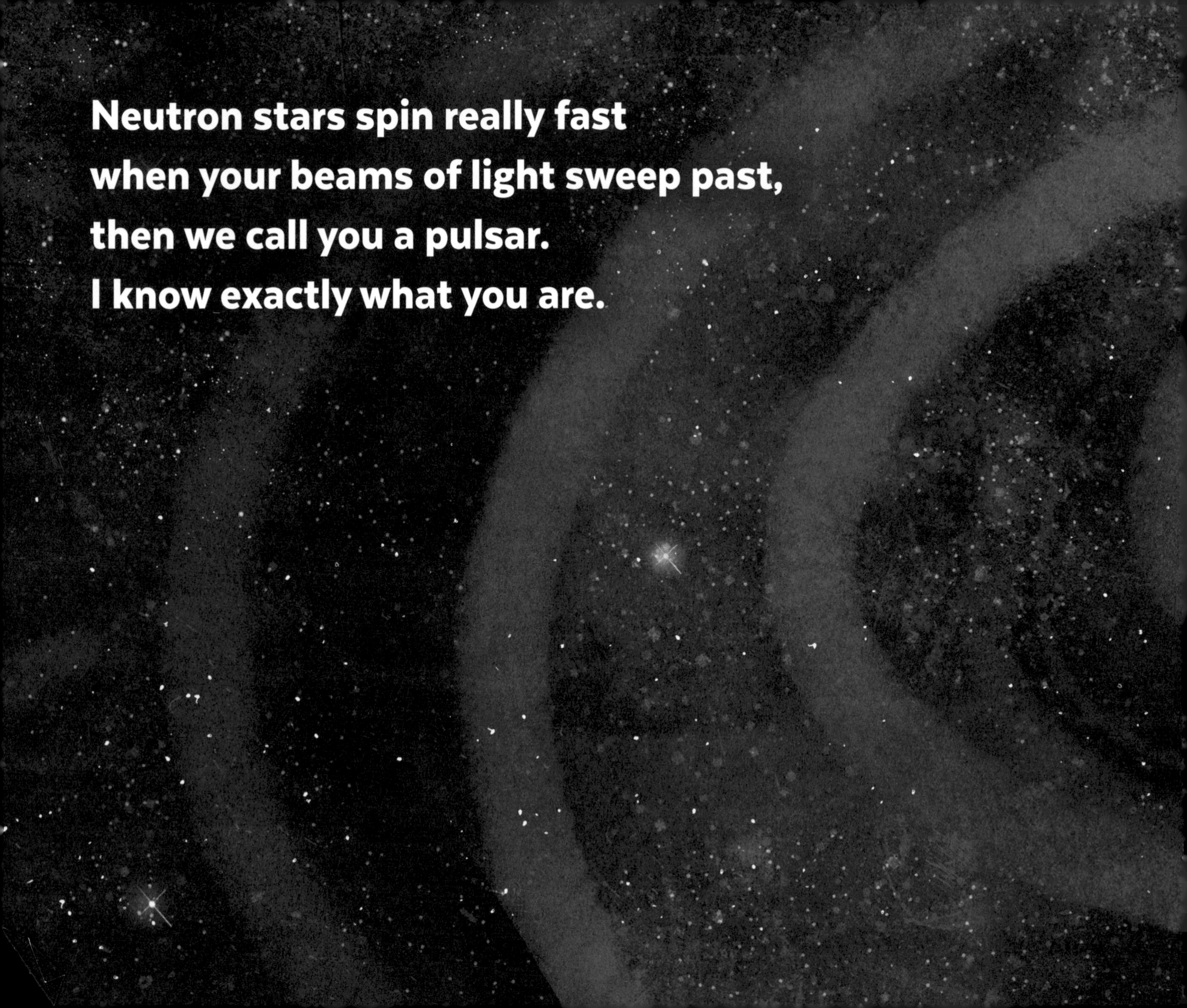

Our Sun's average as stars go,
formed five billion years ago,
halfway through its life so far.
Twinkle midsize yellow star.

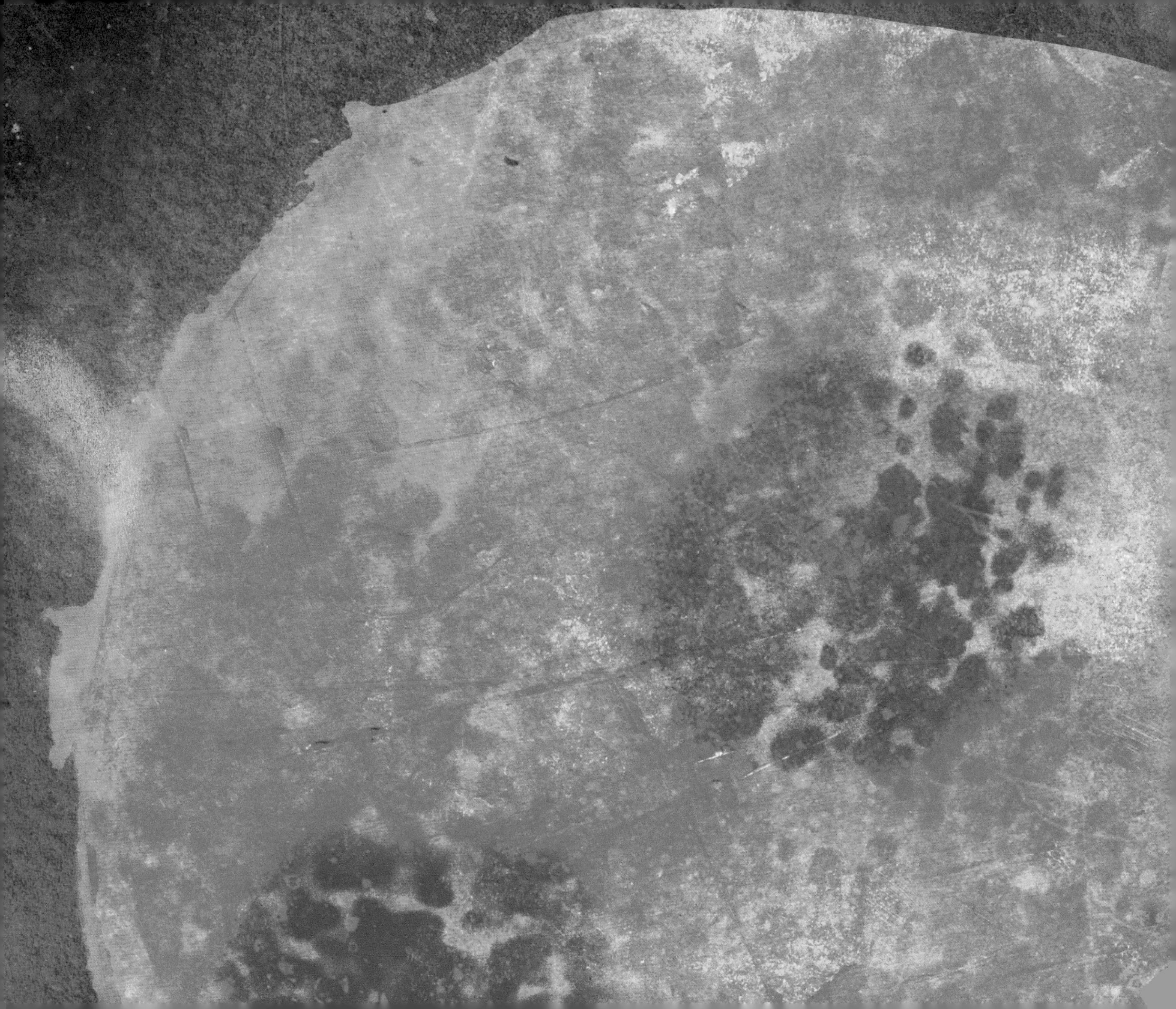

Two stars make a binary,
or a triple if there's three.
Some are solo just like ours.
Twinkle, twinkle, little stars.

Quarter trillion stars all stay
bound within the Milky Way.
Dusty spiral with a bar,
twinkle galaxy of stars.

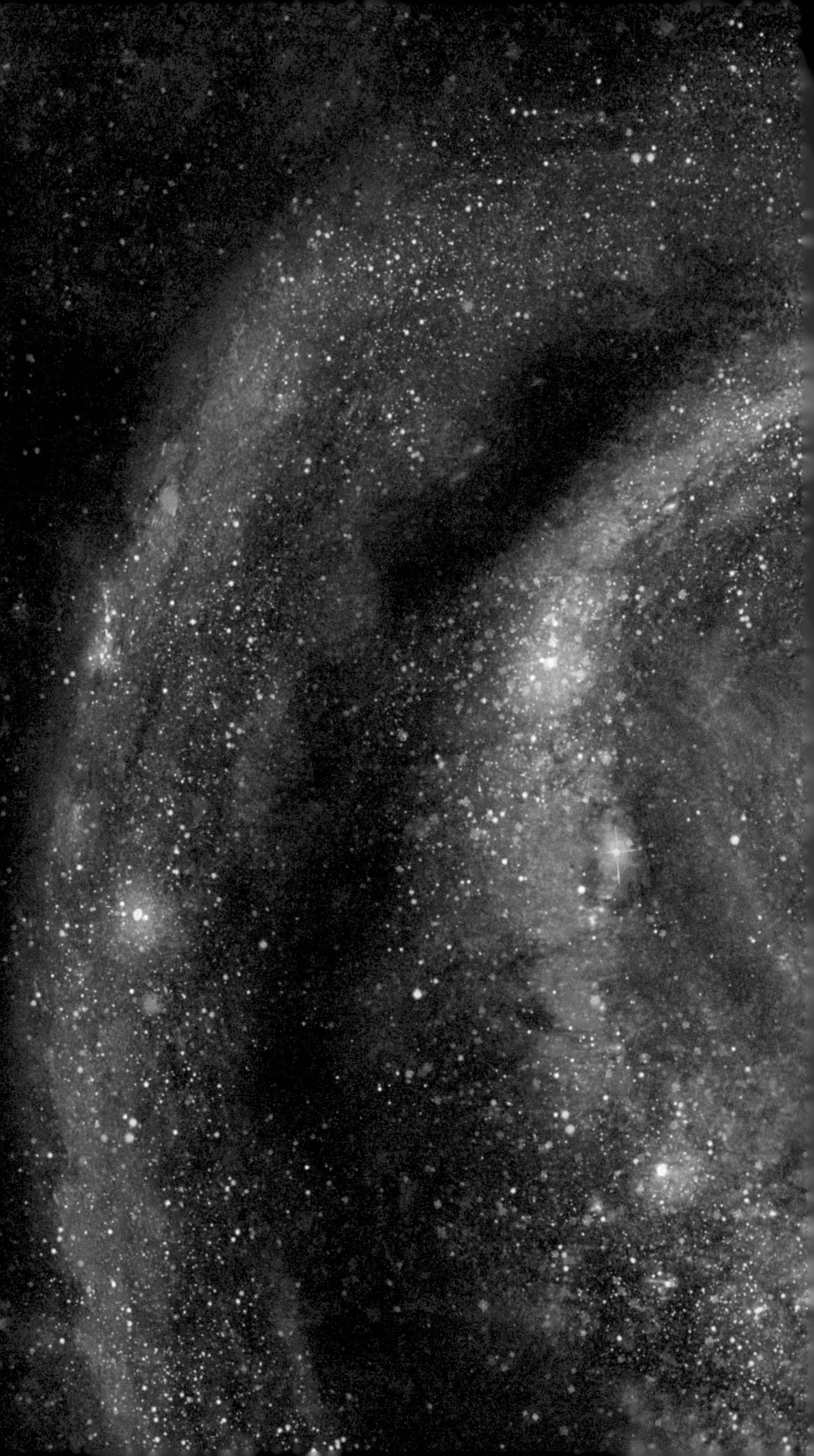

Stars have planets orbiting,
rocky or gaseous, moons and rings.

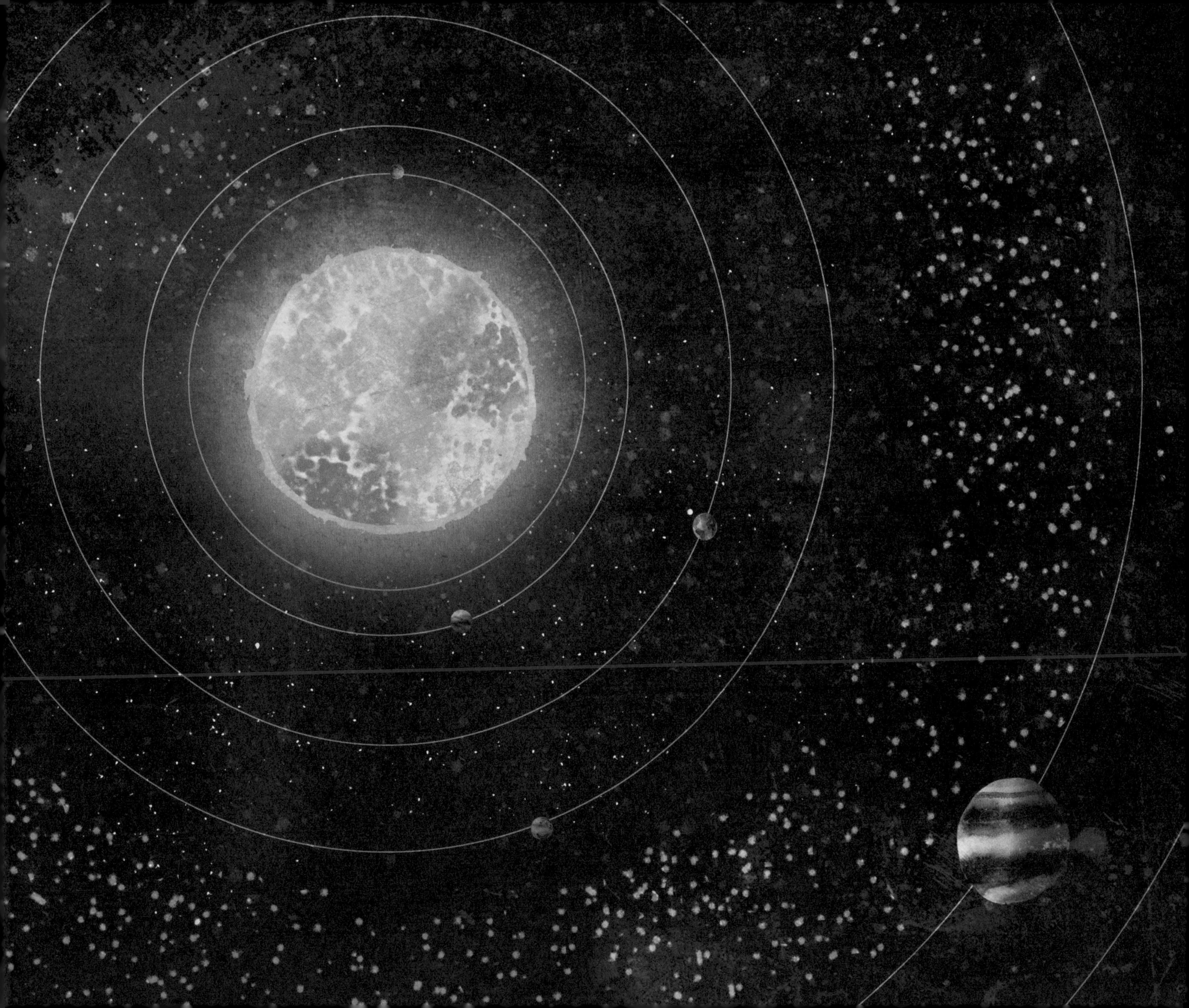

Earth's unique with life so far.
Thank you to our precious star.

Twinkle, twinkle, little star...

I know exactly...

what you are.

A Little More about What Stars Are

Opaque ball of hot dense gas...

What is a star? Stars are huge balls of glowing hot gas—like a balloon, but without the rubber outside holding the gas together. Instead, its own gravity holds it together. Stars are not solid (like rock) or liquid (like water), but wispy gas—kind of like in a cloud, or the air that we breathe, but much hotter. It's so hot that it glows, like a hot burner on an electric stove. Stars glow brightly enough that we can see them very far away. The closest star, our Sun, is a million times larger in size than the Earth, but it looks small to us because it is almost 100 million miles, or 150 million kilometers, away. Proxima Centauri, the next closest star beyond our Sun, is almost 25 trillion (that's 25 million million) miles, or 40 trillion kilometers, away. And the other stars we can see in our night sky are hundreds of times farther still. Even though they are huge like our Sun, they look like tiny points just because of their great distance from Earth.

Constellations are at best...

What is a constellation? Constellations are a projection of our view of the stars that surround our Sun in space, from our unique viewpoint. Two stars that appear close together in one constellation are not necessarily close together in space. One might be much closer to us than another, but just lie almost in the same direction. Various cultures throughout history have grouped the stars that appear near one another into patterns, and made up characters, mythologies, and stories to fit the patterns. Different cultures identified different patterns. Tracking the gradual drifting of these patterns through the sky helped mark the passing of seasons in the year. Today, modern astronomers have divided up the whole sky into 88 agreed-upon constellation areas. Each includes a block of area surrounding a historical constellation. In this system, every possible spot or direction in the sky will fall into one of the 88 areas.

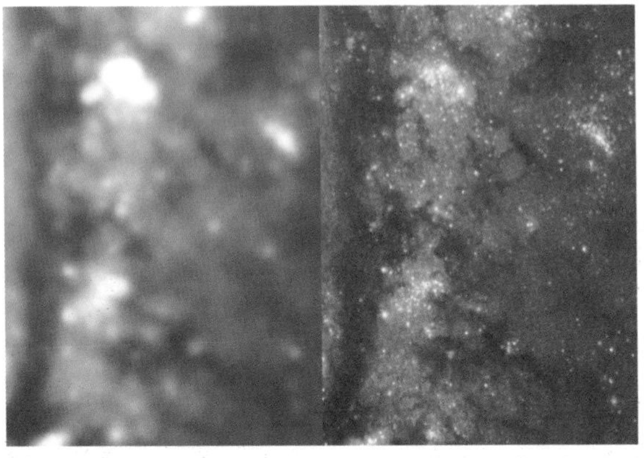

View of another galaxy looking through Earth's atmosphere

View of same galaxy from space, above Earth's atmosphere

Atmospheric turbulence...

What causes twinkling? Stars don't really twinkle. It is actually the turbulent atmosphere of our Earth—which we must look through to see stars, galaxies, etc.—that causes the twinkling effect. The atmosphere slightly ripples and wavers due to convection (hot air rising and cool air falling). When light passes through this moving air, the light gets bent and distorted and causes the starlight to appear to waver and jump around from our perspective. It is a similar effect to looking at an object on the bottom of a swimming pool when the water is sloshing and rippling: the object appears to jump around. But if the pool didn't have water, or if the water were perfectly still, the object wouldn't appear to jump and you could see it clearly. Similarly, if Earth didn't have an atmosphere, or if our atmosphere were perfectly still, stars would not twinkle at all and galaxies wouldn't look as blurry.

Fusing atoms in your core...

What makes stars shine? Stars shine because the elements inside them are undergoing nuclear fusion. This means that the nuclei of the atoms are fusing, or sticking together, and making new atoms. In most stars, including our Sun, hydrogen (the smallest and simplest atom) is being fused to create helium (the next smallest and simplest atom). Small stars can also create a few heavier elements like carbon. Larger stars can create elements that are heavier still like oxygen, neon, and iron. Nearly all the elements on the periodic table of elements were created by nuclear fusion inside of stars, either as they were living, or dying.

Smallest ones burn cool and slow...

Red stars. Small stars look yellow or orange, and the very smallest even look reddish in color. The smallest stars are the most numerous, with larger and larger stars being less and less common in our galaxy. The surface of our Sun, a relatively small star, is about 5,800 Kelvins, which is about 5,500 degrees Celsius, or almost 10,000 degrees Fahrenheit. Inside the core of the star is hotter still: about 15 million degrees Celsius (and Kelvins), or almost 30 million degrees Fahrenheit.

Largest ones are hot and blue...

Blue stars. The larger the star, the hotter the temperature, and the bluer the color. Unlike small stars, which peter out in an anticlimactic cosmic "burp" and remain as gradually fading cinders over eons, large stars die in a dramatic fashion: they explode in a violent and catastrophic supernova, blasting their outer layers of gas into their surroundings. This ejected material replenishes the surrounding space with new gas that can be available for the next generation of stars and planets to form. The core left behind after the supernova is called a neutron star, which can sometimes turn into a black hole if it has enough mass to trigger gravitational collapse.

Gravity holds on too tight...

What is a black hole? A black hole is gravity's ultimate victory. It can form when a neutron star collapses under its own gravity. It has all of the mass of the neutron star (several suns' worth), but it is collapsed down into zero physical size: a mathematical singularity. Although black holes have a perfectly normal amount of mass (just a few times the mass of our Sun), that mass is infinitely compressed, so black holes have infinite density. Thus the gravity very close to a black hole gets stronger and stronger without limit. This is why not even light could escape from very close to a black hole, leading to the name "black."

Neutron stars spin really fast...

What is a neutron star? A neutron star is the leftover core of a high-mass star that died. If it does not continue collapsing to form a black hole, it just remains a neutron star forever. Neutron stars are small (just a few miles or kilometers across) and incredibly dense, with very strong gravity at their surface. This strong gravity allows them to hold themselves together even when they are spinning very rapidly: tens or even hundreds of times per second. Neutron stars emit beams of light out from the poles of their magnetic fields. As the neutron star spins in space, these beams sweep around too. If one of those beams happens to sweep past Earth and repeatedly point at us briefly during each sweeping circuit, we would see a brief pulse of light once per rotation and we would call that neutron star a "pulsar."

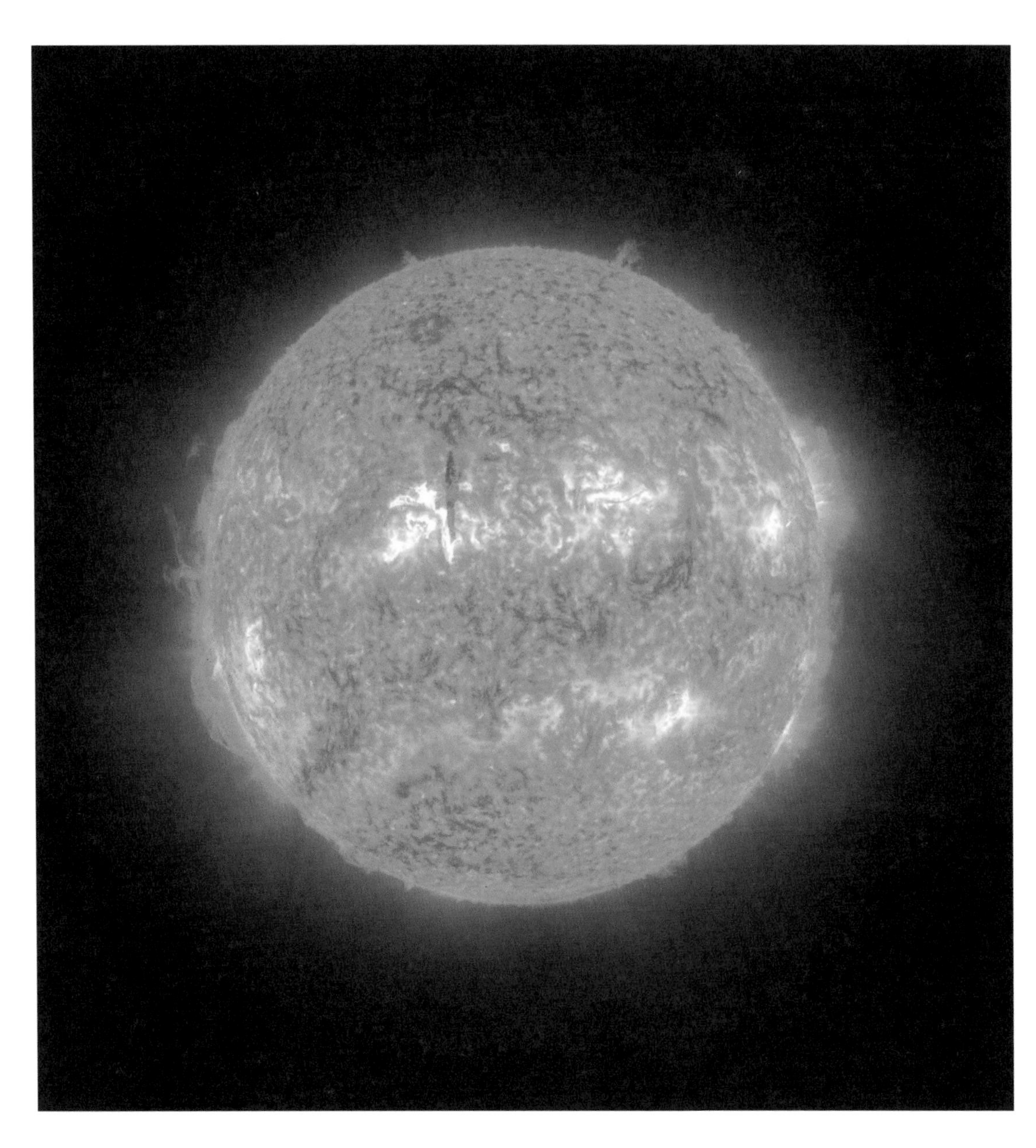

Our Sun's average as stars go...

What is our Sun? Our Sun is a medium-small sized star. We tend to think of our Sun as yellow, but that is a result of seeing its light through Earth's atmosphere. Our atmosphere filters out some of the bluer colors thus making the Sun look more yellow. In outer space, our Sun would look pure white. Our Sun's total expected lifetime estimate, based on the amount of hydrogen fuel that it has available, is about 10 billion years. Since our Sun formed a little over 4.5 billion years ago (which is also the age of the Earth), it has about 5 billion years left to go.

Two stars make a binary...

What is a binary? When two stars orbit one another, they are called a binary system. If one of the stars is much larger than the other, they still orbit one another, but the larger star stays closer to the middle and the smaller star swings in a larger orbit around it. The two stars in a binary system always stay on opposite sides of their "center of mass," or imaginary center balance point—like the fulcrum of a seesaw. Many stars exist in such pairs, or even larger groups.

Quarter trillion stars all stay...

What is a galaxy? A galaxy is a huge group of stars plus all the intervening gas and dust that is the raw material for new stars, that all stay in the same collection due to their mutual gravitational attraction. The stars, gas, and dust are all orbiting around one another in a big swirling system. There is plenty of space between the individual stars, so they hardly ever run into one another. The galaxy we live in is called the Milky Way. Our Sun is just one of a few hundred billion stars. Many of the stars are clumped along spiral arms that trace out a pinwheel shape in the galaxy, with the spiral arms joined in the middle with a straight section called a bar.

Stars have planets orbiting...

Planets. Our solar system has eight major planets, several dwarf planets, and innumerable minor planets, asteroids, comets, etc., that are all orbiting our star, the Sun. Many of the other stars we see in the night sky have one or more of their own planets too. We have found planets around thousands of stars so far, with more discoveries all the time. Planets can come in a variety of sizes and compositions in our solar system, ranging from small solid ("rocky") planets like Mars to large

puffy soft ("gaseous") planets like Jupiter. At least in our solar system, these large gaseous planets tend to have lots of moons and rings surrounding the planet, while the small rocky planets tend to have few or no moons and no rings. But of all the thousands of planets discovered so far, including the few within our solar system and the many beyond, no other worlds except for Earth have been shown to host life forms of any kind.